FLYING START

SWIMMING

Jim Noble

The Bookwright Press
New York • 1991

Flying Start

Titles in this series

Fishing	Running
Gymnastics	Soccer
Judo	Swimming

Words in **bold** in the text are explained in the glossary on page 30.

Cover: Janet Evans, who won several Olympic gold medals for swimming.

First published in the
United States in 1991 by
The Bookwright Press
387 Park Avenue South
New York, NY 10016

First published in 1991 by
Wayland (Publishers) Ltd
61 Western Rd, Hove
East Sussex BN3 1JD, England

Library of Congress Cataloging-in-Publication Data
Noble, Jim.
    Swimming/Jim Noble.
        p.   cm. — (Flying start)
    Includes bibliographical references and index.
    Summary: All the advantages of learning how to swim are presented
together with the correct terminology for competition swimming.
    ISBN 0-531-18466-8
    1. Swimming – Juvenile literature.   [1. Swimming.]   I. Title.
II. Series.
GV837.6.N63   1991   91-6314
797.2'1 – dc20   CIP
                                                                   AC

Typesetter: Dorchester Typesetting Group Ltd
Printer: Casterman S.A., Belgium.

CONTENTS

SINK OR SWIM?

If you can swim there are many exciting things to do. You can learn to dive, to swim underwater and to do handstands or somersaults. You can learn new strokes and play water games with your friends. If you want to surf or windsurf you need to be able to swim.

At many pools there are clubs you can join, to learn how to play water polo or become a **synchronized swimmer**.

Once you can swim, you will be able to go into wave pools like this one.

If you want to go windsurfing or surfing it is very important to be able to swim well.

Water polo is a game for two teams, with seven players in each team. The aim is to score by throwing the ball into the other team's goal. You use a soccer-sized ball, and passes and shots must be made using one hand.

Synchronized swimmers perform routines in the water in the same way dancers do on land. They try to keep in time with each other and with the music they perform to.

For many people, taking part in races is very exciting. All important swimming races are held in pools that are either 82 or 164 feet (25 or 50 m) long. These pools are divided into lanes. The biggest pools have eight lanes.

A big swimming race is really exciting. When it is about to begin the racers go to their lanes. When the starter says, "Take your marks" the swimmers step to the front of their **starting blocks**.

Below Swimming pools that people race in are divided up into lanes.

The swimmers bend down into a starting position. When they have all stopped moving, the starting signal is given.

The starting signal can be a loud whistle or a shot from a starting pistol. Other signals are a shout of "Go!" or the sound of a loud electronic "beep."

At the start of a race, swimmers dive off the starting blocks. The signal for this is usually a gun going off. The cord from this gun runs to each block, and sets off a loud "beep" instead of a "bang."

Then the swimmers dive in and the race is on! Different judges make sure that the swimmers are doing the stroke right and turning around correctly at the end of each length. Using **stopwatches**, timekeepers in each lane take the time of each swimmer. Once the race is over judges rank the swimmers in order.

At important competitions, such as the **Olympic Games**, **automatic timing** equipment is used to find out swimmers' times.

The race is on! There are lots of different ways to dive in, as you can see from this picture.

The special pads at the end of the pool have sent a message to a giant scoreboard to tell everyone that this swimmer has won.

At the end of the pool there are special pads that record when they have been touched. As each swimmer touches the end of the pool, the pad sends a signal to a computer. The computer figures out each swimmer's time.

All the swimmers' times, and their places in the race, are then shown on a giant scoreboard for everyone to see.

HOW TO BEGIN

Before you start to swim you must be able to push and glide. When you are learning, wearing arm floats might help to give you confidence.

First, try learning about how to push and glide with arm floats on. Stand quite close to the side of the pool. Take a deep breath, put your face in the water and push toward the poolside.

Practicing pushing off and gliding will help your swimming lessons.

When you feel safe doing this, move farther away from the side of the pool. Then you can take off the arm floats and try gliding without them on.

Later on, try pushing and gliding away from the poolside. When you want to stand up, press down with your hands, tuck your knees in and lift up your head. Once you are upright put your feet on the bottom of the pool. Next try pushing and gliding on your back. The pictures below show you how.

Once you can glide on your front, try doing it on your back.

When you can push and glide, you will be ready to learn one of the swimming strokes. Look at pages 12 to 14 to find out how.

Breaststroke is a useful stroke to learn, because you can see where you are going easily. It can be swum quite a long way without making you tired. This is because you can rest your arms and legs between strokes.

Below Breaststroke.

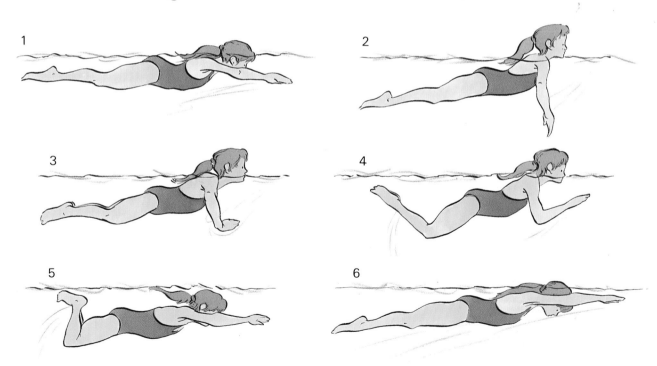

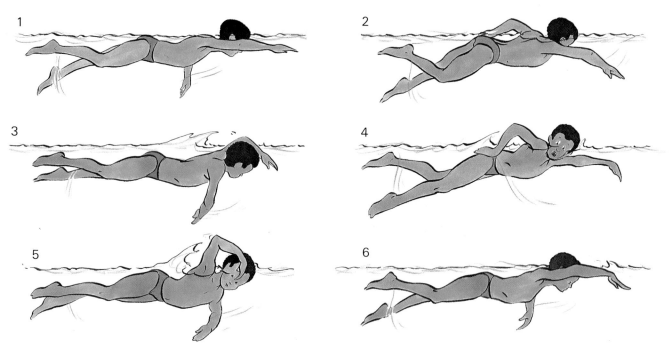

You might find that you like backstroke more. Because your face is out of the water, breathing is easier.

Front crawl is usually called freestyle. Although you are allowed to swim any stroke in freestyle races, people always swim front crawl because it is the fastest stroke! As in backstroke your arms and legs have to move all the time.

Above Front crawl.

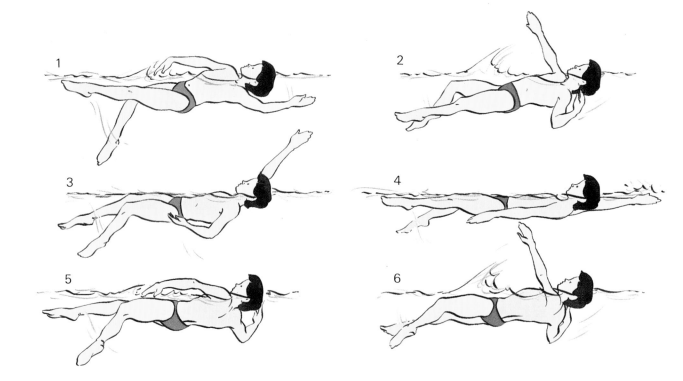

In all these strokes you should try to keep your body as **streamlined** as possible. But try to make sure your legs stay below the surface.

If you are taking part in a sport such as sailing or surfing, it is very useful to know how to **tread water**. Stand in water up to your shoulders. Wear arm floats or hold a **floatboard** under each arm.

Above Back stroke.
Below Stay streamlined.

First lift both feet off the bottom. Then press downward with your feet as if you were walking upstairs. Doing this will keep you afloat in an upright position. Use the picture below as a guide.

Another way of treading water is to do a breaststroke kick with your legs and move your hands in small circles. Once you can tread water in one of these ways, try it without arm floats or floatboards.

Above Water polo players have to be good at treading water, so they can throw the ball.

Treading water is a bit like running, except you do not go anywhere.

GETTING IN

Once you can stay afloat easily, why not try some simple dives? The picture below shows the kneeling dive. From the position shown in the picture, lean forward and try to touch the water. As you overbalance into the water, keep your head between your arms and aim to dive outward and downward.

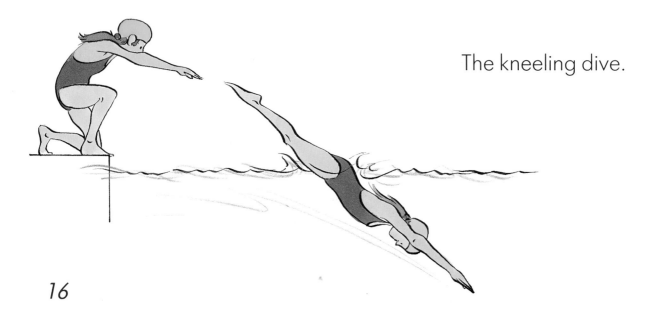

The kneeling dive.

Make sure the water is deep enough before you dive in, or you will bang your head! For the dives shown here the water should be at least 5 feet (1½ m) deep.

The lunge dive.

In the lunge dive (shown above) you first bend forward. Lifting one leg behind you and keeping your body straight will cause you to overbalance. If you keep your body straight and stretched and try to dive out as well as down, you will be able to do a very **clean dive**.

17

The plunge dive.

The plunge dive (above) is similar to a racing dive. Start by leaning forward. As you start to overbalance, swing your arms forward and push off strongly with your legs. Keep your body stretched out until you come back up to the surface.

If the water hurts your eyes, you can wear goggles. But make sure you put the **eyepiece** on first. Hold it in place and then stretch the

Put the eyepiece of the goggles on first.

rubber strap over the back of your head. Otherwise the eyepiece will spring back and hurt your eyes, which will spoil your swim!

These swimmers at the 1988 Seoul Olympics are all expert divers.

FLYING START FITNESS

To swim well you need to be fit. One of the best ways of getting fit is to do distance swims. At first you will probably not be able to swim far.

These distance swimmers are taking part in a race in the sea in France.

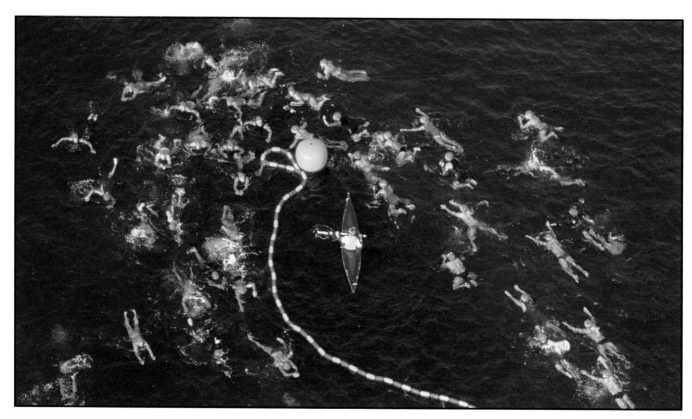

Try to swim a little farther each time you visit the pool. Each time you will get a little more fit.

Most swimmers warm up before they get in the pool. This is to make sure that they do not strain their muscles. Here are a few easy exercises that swimmers find useful. When you are doing them make sure that you can feel your muscles stretching, but not too much or you will hurt yourself.

Above and **below**
Windmills are a good warm up for swimming.

Windmills

Standing with your feet apart, begin backward circling with one arm, then the other. Then do it with both arms at the same time. Do this eight or ten times. Then do the same number of forward circles. The picture on the right shows you how to do this exercise.

Shoulder stretching

Stand quite close to a chair. Put your wrists on the back of the chair. Slowly press your chest downward until you can feel the strain in your shoulders, then slowly straighten up.

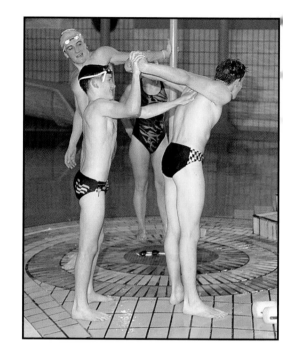

Above and **above left** It is important for swimmers to have flexible shoulders.

Left Bendy body exercises are very useful for swimmers. Do this one five or six times.

Bendy body

Stand with your hands on your hips. Keep your body upright and your legs straight, and bend to the left and then to the right, as shown below left. Make sure you can feel your sides being stretched. Repeat this ten or twelve times for each side of your body. The extra flexibility will be good for your swimming.

Forward reaching

Sit on the floor with your legs straight and apart as the picture on the right shows. Reach forward and try to touch your left foot with your right hand. Stop when you can feel the muscles in the back of your leg stretching. Then try to touch your right foot with your left hand. Do this six or eight times.

Below Forward reaching is very good for your leg muscles.

THE GREAT RACE

Today's famous swimmers have been training for as long as ten years. They train for four or more hours a day, almost every day of the week! When the day of competition arrives they need to be in **peak form.**

Let us go back in time. To a day that was a very special one for one swimmer . . . Adrian Moorhouse.

This is the moment he has been waiting for. Years of training have earned him a place in the most important race he has ever been in — the Olympic 100-meter breaststroke final. He has won a gold medal in nearly every championship apart from the Olympic Games.

Hours of training go into the performances of great swimmers.

The opening ceremony at the Los Angeles Olympics. The Olympics is the competition that all sportspeople would love to win.

Standing behind their blocks are seven other **finalists**. Each is a brilliant swimmer. Every one of them hopes to win the gold medal. The **referee** blows several short blasts on his whistle. He checks that they are all ready. One long blast and the eight swimmers get on their blocks and stand at the back. The referee raises his hand. The starter takes over. On the words "Take your marks" all eight step forward and bend down into the starting position. When they have stopped moving, the starting signal is given.

In one line all eight plunge into the water. The race has begun! As they come to the surface they are almost in a line. But after one length a swimmer has moved in front and there are two close behind him. The favorite is in sixth place, 6 yards (2 m) behind. With 160 feet (50 m) to go he has to swim the race of his life!

Powering his way through the water he starts to catch up. Thirty feet (9 m) from the finish he has moved up into third place.

Half-way through the Olympic final the favorite was in sixth place. Could he close the gap?

Suddenly he **surges** up to the two in front. In a very close finish he touches the end of the pool first. The British supporters are on their feet. They are whistling and cheering. Adrian Moorhouse has won! He is the 1988 Olympic 100-meter breaststroke champion.

The joy of winning an Olympic gold medal is easy to see in this picture of Adrian Moorhouse.

Imagine you are in your first race. When you come to compete, you will probably feel very nervous. Try to remember that even world champion swimmers have "butterflies" before a race.

To keep from worrying too much, and to get ready for the race, swimmers often sit quietly and imagine how the race will go. They imagine themselves swimming really well, turning fast and sprinting to the finish. Try not to imagine yourself swimming very slowly, or you probably will!

When the gun goes off try to do a really good dive. Do not start too fast or you will have no energy left at the end of the race. It is always good to have a little bit left for the final **sprint**. Try to swim smoothly and breathe regularly. When you turn and finish make sure you do it right.

Just before the race, sit quietly and imagine how it will go.

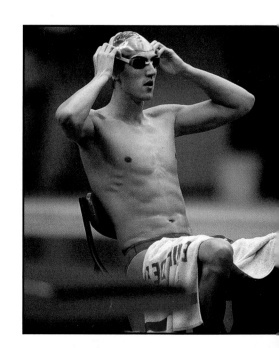

Make sure that you finish really fast – many people lose races because they slow down at the very end.

Whatever the result is, the important thing is to do your best. It does not matter if you do not win. If you have really tried as hard as you can, you should be very proud of yourself. But remember, if you do want to win, training hard is the only sure way to success!

Training really hard is the only way to be sure that you will win races.

923333

Glossary

Automatic timing Timing device that works without a person watching and controlling it.

Clean dive A clean dive is one in which as little splash as possible is made.

Eyepiece The part of the goggles made of plastic lenses, through which you can see.

Finalist A person who qualifies for a final after taking part in earlier qualifying races.

Floatboard A support made of light, floating material. It helps you to stay on the surface.

Olympic Games A sports competition held every four years in which the world's best athletes compete.

Peak form The best possible physical condition.

Referee The person in charge of a swimming race.

Sprint High speed over a short distance.

Starting block A raised platform from which swimmers dive into the water in a race.

Stopwatch A watch used for timing very accurately.

Streamlined Something that has a smooth shape that helps it go through the water easily is streamlined.

Surge To move forward more quickly than the other racers.

Synchronized swimming Movements to music that two or more swimmers perform in time with each other.

Tread water To keep upright in the water, using leg and arm movements.

Books about swimming

Berridge, Celia, *Going Swimming,* Look and Learn Books, 1987.

Chiefari and Wightman, *Better Synchronized Swimming for Boys and Girls,* Putnam, 1981.

Gutman, B., *Go For It: Swimming,* Grey Castle, 1989.

Kolbisen, I., *Starfish Floats and Motorboats: A Child's Primer for Beginning Swimming,* I Think I Can, 1989.

Reiter, John, ed., *Wiggle-Butts and Up-Faces: A Child's Primer for Beginning Swimming,* I Think I Can, 1989.

Sanborn, L., and L. Eberhardt, *Swim Free,* Search Public, 1982.

Winter, Ginny L., *Swimming Book,* Astor-Honor, 1964.

World of Sports Series, *Swimming and Diving,* Silver Burdett, 1988.

YMCA of the U.S.A., *Splash: YMCA Progressive Swimming,* Human Kinetics, 1986.

The next step

Contact your local chapter of the American Red Cross for low-cost swimming lessons in your area.

United States Swimming, Inc.
1750 E. Boulder St.
Colorado Springs, CO 80909

Index

Numbers in **bold** indicate pictures or artwork as well as text.

Picture Acknowledgments

All artwork was provided by Peter Parr.
All-Sport *cover*, 4, 6 (Tony Duffy), 7 (top, Michael King), 9 (Simon Bruty), 15 (Pascal Rondeau), 19 (Simon Bruty), 20 (Vandystadt), 25 (Steve Powell), 26 (Simon Bruty), 27 (Tony Duffy); Eye Ubiquitous (Paul Seheult) 14, 18, 21, 22, 24, 29; Sporting Pictures 7, 8.